The Poor Man
In
The Flesh

ELMA MITCHELL

HARRY CHAMBERS/PETERLOO POETS

First published in 1976
by Harry Chambers/Peterloo Poets
8 Cavendish Road, Heaton Mersey, Stockport SK4 3DN, Cheshire

ISBN 0 905291 04 2

NEW ADDRESS

HARRY CHAMBERS/PETERLOO POETS
Treovis Farm Cottage, Upton Cross,
Liskeard, Cornwall PL14 5BQ

Printed in Great Britain by
The Scolar Press Limited, Ilkley, Yorkshire

THE POOR MAN IN THE FLESH

This first collection includes recent poems plus the best from two earlier unpublished groups, both of which won Camden Festival prizes. These are poems of contemporary everyday work and leisure. Poems in this collection deal with various occupations, vocations and preoccupations, including those suggested by the title of an earlier group of poems—*18 Ways Of Being A Woman.*

ACKNOWLEDGEMENTS are due to the editors of *The New States-man*, *Outposts*, *P.E.N. New Poems 1967*, *Phoenix*, and *Anon.* (U.S.A.), in whose pages some of these poems have previously appeared.

"Thoughts After Ruskin" has been broadcast on South African Radio.

The frontispiece/cover photograph of a *Male Head** is reproduced from the catalogue of the Romano-British Sculptures in the Gloucester City collection by kind permission of the Curator of the Gloucester City Museum.

Male Head: Height 8″. Found in 1934 during excavations for an extension to the rear of the Bon Marché store. The hair-style, with a fringe of short crescent-shaped locks, dates this piece to the first few decades of the Roman occupation. The high forehead, the three-dimensional build and the whole idea of monumental stone sculpture are derived from continental Roman art; but, as is natural in a work of this date, the other features of the head are more reminiscent of pre-Roman British art. This head may have surmounted a body of stone or wood, now lost. It may, on the other hand, have surmounted a bust carved from the top of a squared block of stone. Complete monuments of this kind have been found in France, and according to the mediaeval *Life Of St. Patrick* they were worshipped as idols.

To Micky and Jenny, with love

CONTENTS

The Poor Man In The Flesh

The poor man in the flesh
   At ninety-eight-point-four
Envisages his parallel
   Living above the economic floor,
Who kissed the Cypriot, and has no need to snore.

He comes on wings of swan
   Above the staggering buses,
Not netted in the streets; beyond
   Requests and terminuses,
Bending his wits and limbs to superhuman uses.

Under the uniformity of hats,
   Within the convolutions of the brain,
Pedestrians visit pomegranates;
   The patient faces in the rain
Have been as far as Troy, and back again.

The plain man in the train
   Bound to his home and supper,
Reading the poets like a school-room secret
   In camouflage of newspaper,
Is keeping dark his sleeping-partner
And only proper peer, Apollo the Far-Darter.

Thoughts After Ruskin

Women reminded him of lilies and roses.
Me they remind rather of blood and soap,
Armed with a warm rag, assaulting noses,
Ears, neck, mouth and all the secret places:

Armed with a sharp knife, cutting up liver,
Holding hearts to bleed under a running tap,
Gutting and stuffing, pickling and preserving,
Scalding, blanching, broiling, pulverising,
—All the terrible chemistry of their kitchens.

Their distant husbands lean across mahogany
And delicately manipulate the market,
While safe at home, the tender and the gentle
Are killing tiny mice, dead snap by the neck,
Asphyxiating flies, evicting spiders,
Scrubbing, scouring aloud, disturbing cupboards,
Committing things to dustbins, twisting, wringing,
Wrists red and knuckles white and fingers puckered,
Pulpy, tepid. Steering screaming cleaners
Arounds the snags of furniture, they straighten
And haul out sheets from under the incontinent
And heavy old, stoop to importunate young,
Tugging, folding, tucking, zipping, buttoning,
Spooning in food, encouraging excretion,
Mopping up vomit, stabbing cloth with needles,
Contorting wool around their knitting needles,
Creating snug and comfy on their needles.

Their huge hands! their everywhere eyes! their voices
Raised to convey across the hullabaloo,

Their massive thighs and breasts dispensing comfort,
Their bloody passages and hairy crannies,
Their wombs that pocket a man upside down!

And when all's over, off with overalls,
Quickly consulting clocks, they go upstairs,
Sit and sigh a little, brushing hair,
And somehow find, in mirrors, colours, odours,
Their essences of lilies and of roses.

Station Exit

A day of eight hours, in the clerkly concrete,
Has left me all unfit for the clouds' proportions
Over Blackheath, and the softly summoning blossoms.

The cheeky blackbird says whatever he pleases,
Not having set himself to gain these prizes,
Which tie me to the rails, which fix my hat,

A settled citizen, with no wind blowing,
And upright smirk, unlike the grasses' bowing.

The Corset

The corset came today. I cannot wear it.

What are your difficulties, may I ask?
A slight constriction round about the heart?
That, at your time of life, you must expect,
The back and shoulders mainly take the weight,
Astonishingly comfortable, on the whole
And really very stylish,—for your size.
This line is very flattering to the bust,
And this delineates what was once a waist,
And further down, you see, complete control . .

You'll soon acquire the knack; just slip it on,
Wriggle, distort, contract—that's right, that's it.
Now you are one smooth mould from head to thighs.
You'll be surprised how good it makes you feel . .

The corset came today. I will not wear it.
Come, lumpish lumbering muscles, to your task,
Unsupple wits, turn sinuous again,
Or live as limp and cripple, but let live.

Cripple Song

Touch iron, it's cold.
Clutch iron, it bites
The hand that feels it.

Iron holds me up.

Bracing, biting, dragging,
With clitter-clatter,
Like a swung sword, modelled for no hero,
Like a shod plough, tipped for no fruition,

Iron holds me up.

Some part of me that limps and falls
Cries when it falls and feels
The rest is iron.

The rest is iron.

The Idiot Boy

The nasty child, the horrid one
Sits in a corner, rocking to and fro,
Sucking his thumb and staring into air.

The horrid child, the nasty one,
We hate him so, we hate him so,
Because, when we attack, he isn't there.

2

The Lord created me a sponge,
He did. And I
Live out my faculties as best I can
Without a hand
Without an eye.

Bask I can
My sprawling gathering glory in the green,
The glide;
I wamble with the waxing, waning tide,
Among the bubbles and the mouths
As compassless we journey, north and south.

To all my scaled and crusted ancestors
I raise my fungus hat.
The weeds of slime have leave to loiter
Unprovoked around my sucking throat.

My water world, it tilts, it slips,
It rocks with me, it rocks,
I live here, in the lurch,
I never search
The hard flat surface for the talking ships.

Portrait In A Passport
Age: 16

Abashed to have a toffee in her mouth
At the perpetuating click, she sulks.
Hungry, but not so ignorant as she looks.

Too little chin, redundancy of nose:
Bit of a refugee, as who is not,
When the alternatives begin to close.

Top-heavy girl—the legs are out of sight.
This drooping face, in mourning for its dolls,
Gave logic the once-over, and sits tight.

Nature will come along and put things right,
The doctor said, consulted about spots,
Passing the buck to nameless genitals.

This was a good deal simpler than the truth.

Go anywhere, do anything: this face
Had still no visa for its native place.

Travel Agent

Selling for ten fat years the hunted sun,
He bathed, every day, in vicarious pleasures,
Hot in his telephone ear, he heard the mermaids
Always just off the map, but splashing, singing,
Waiting for him; he held the world in his fingers,
The oceans caught in his network of air, the land
Laced with his routes, his tours, his dream hotels . . .

The new regulations have caused a stillness, a silence,
The need for a little adjustment. His business is
To make these little adjustments.

Stay where you are, they said to him, be what you have
Become in the years of the chair and the lurid brochure,
The poster's allure; your eyes, your tongue, your voice,
Your choice of what, in the main, to do with your day,
Not economics it was put you to sit, here at the telephone's end,
Nor politics, wife, mother, nor other devil projected
From the inside out; come now, come, begin—
This time you have bought your own ticket, and the escape
Literature you have commissioned is all you will have to rely on.

Hold very tight; fasten your belt; the real
Journey begins to lift, up from the dead ground,
Here, now and screaming.

Walking Alone

Our houses stand apart, and so
The time had come I had to go
Out from the fire, into the snow
—He would have come, but I said No.

I walk beyond the lights I know,
The busy poet's harmless glow,
The lovers curtained from the snow
—He would have come, but I said No.

No voices on the winds that blow,
No light house in the swivelling snow,
No flare, no flame, the way I go
—But heel and toe, and heel and toe.

Shepherd At Work

MAN
Old and cold and creaky-boned among
The first, creased lambs,
But strong: look at his thighs, his hands.

Knowing what is to do
Among the struggle of the ewes
To pack and unpack their wombs,

Relentless and compassionate
Propagator: liberator:
Doctor and comforter,

Dumb beast among dumb beasts,
He takes the hills in his stride,
The sheltering stones his colleagues.

The wind is his, and the aches of the long day,
The market, the cash, the alarms, the turning-out,
The will to birth out of the barren cold.

Blood on his hands; sweat on his head;
Salvation on two weary legs,
A night of counting sheep.

DOGS
Two tumbling, juggling dogs
Pour like water over the rough of the landscape.
Working as his interpreters,

19

They crouch, magnetic,
Holding in the sheep
And held by them.

These words are paraphrases
Of the far more precise
Diction of whistles and of cries

Conveyed to alerted ears, acknowledging tails,
And sentient intelligence
Housed in a soft and feline poise.

Their action, instant silk
Solicitude of sheep,
Between the briar and the rock.
Once home, they will eat meat.

SHEEP
We, we
Bollop along meekly, under instruction,
Wool-gathering,
Dense with fleece.

But, but,
(Stay together, my brothers; turn together
To face the enemy)
We have seen the dog, the black
And creeping doom,
And our god, walking.

Mais, mais,
(Our language is all hair, all crying)
We live more bleating free than either
Two legs worrying, or
Four legs creeping and crawling.

Munch, munch,
Between the sea and sky,
At the heather line,
Scattered and stout as rocks,
All winter we survive

To make at last
Your twin-set and your vest,
Your butcher's holiday.

Bite, bite,
Remember us, among the central heating
And mint-sauced eating,
Remember us,
The straining of the ewes,
The regal rams,
The walking wool-sacks, and
The snow-dropped lambs,

Bite, bite,
All day, all night,
Shift, nibble and sleep.
The proper study of sheep.

Plain Jane

One year on fire I had, and all the rest
Plain Jane,
Dust-pan and brush,
The tinkle of the keys
That lock my days.

I fatten, and grow gray,
I wear no ring, I have no say.
Some words indeed remain
But they,
Turning and churning in the single mind
With no respond,
Wear out and fray.

The closet has its moth,
The key, its rub and rust;
I take my shopping-basket, brisk
To do my daily best.

Among the choice of biscuits, the pick of the meat,
I once again prefer
This one to that
And pay

And on my way.

Fisher Willie In Hospital

Not, as he seems, asleep,
Eyeshut he lies and sees
No fluorescent strip
But restlessness of water
Where the brown, bladdering weed
Shaggies the reef.

He is drawing up the nets
Made of remembering
Full of thinking fish.
Now he is hooked, gaffed
Laid on a table.

Instead of skin
Cold scales
And motion under water,
Heavy, dim
Out of the buzz of Sister and of Doctor.

The visitors recede;
He turns, relieved,
To father salt and mother water,
Effortless, pendant fish
Glide under his lids.

Unable to deploy
The deep, simple skills
Where boat grazes jetty,
Willie wants no pity,
Takes in, emits, liquid,
Asks for a fag, smiles,

Closes his eyes
Without further parley
And is possessed by the sea
In all his groaning channels
And rides a tidal bed.

It was the fish who died.

Alice Uglier

Alice is uglier now by several years.
    Her eyes
Are sunk and fortified against surprise,
    Humiliations, tears.
Sensible to the bone, her gait proclaims.
      Her cut
Of coat disdains the sympathiser, but
    Her mouth is restless: tensions dug
    These trenches in her throat.

She wasn't bred on love or promises,
    Lonely, never alone,
Her future was provided for, not cherished.
    She nursed
Her nearest through senility and worse.
    Placid in gratitude, dumb to abuse,
    She kept
The business out of debt, the books in order,
    But now, it seems, the monkey's loose,
And something's tearing papers in the cellar
    Far down.

While habit, like a well-maintained machine,
    Keeps up the play of knife and fork
And answers questions in between—
    Her sturdy tree is withered to a rod.
She's given up her country walks,
    (Too stiff to stoop for primroses)
Under the table, foot and fist
    Tap out their private messages—
She wakes in darkness to her bath of flames
    And wonders what became of God.

Still,
She must get back, or she'll be missed
   Over the coffee, she'll insist
We should go fifty-fifty on the bill.

This is a block that salts will not remove.
   I pour out coffee, and retain
Her drowning image, and my useless love.

The Need For Coal

There's warmth beneath the earth
Where hope and coal lie buried.
My fingers this cold morning
Are itching to be digging.

Above my ignorant head
Hangs the heavy crust
Of houses, fields and children,
Of gaping hearths, and waiting women,
And round me bones lie lost,
Among the treacherous dust,
The precious dust.

My ghost, sun-glorified soldier,
Marches and sings in Africa
I hear him from the pit.

Deep heart, I have come back,
But not for these or those,
Furnaces, houses, women, fields or children
Whose weight distorts my spine,
Nor for the many many many words
(Which I have heard before)
Which suffocate my lungs.

To you I have come back
Where strength is my incentive
In the strait narrow bed
And close encounter,
Take, take,
My thrusting pick,

My earth-upholding shoulder
Is over you as a lover.

I have come back
To lie and wrestle with you in the darkness
O my black mistress.

. . . *Semper Femina*

Under the hedgerow keep it green,
   Or sparrowed in the park,
A stranger to *The Times;* unseen
   And gentle in the dark,

A haystack love, a wayside love,
   A Venus' wanton boy,
No Vicar, registrar, nor ring
   Confines our flowing joy.

Peaceful sits your sleeping head,
   And weak it is in me,
To dream, beyond the flaming bed,
   The kitchen and the key.

The Prophet

I take the measure of the pyramids
And dodge the trams.
I am the stone the builders have neglected
Under Hungerford Bridge.
With time and Thames I flow
Beside the unhurried Liffey and the Mersey,
My voice is heard in Liverpool and London
And Birmingham beheld my massive silence.

I am Daniel, in the den of Lyon's,
I shall arise, out of the public library,
The first of them that sleep.

Jeune Fille

Then, I spread my dress,
Myself in front of mirror,
Nannie said, Be good,
Her loss is for ever.

I wipe the dirty floor
Now, with a dirty cloth,
Great, striding man has come,
God has gone off.

Odysseus Home

Not sorry to be back,
Had enough glory,
Troy, the Cyclops and the rest,
A hoary story.
The annual re-union with the boys
Fine while it lasts, but mostly noise.
Homeward, homeward lies
My singing joy.

I take the daily train
From love to discipline and back again
I mend the leaks, and lay aside
Coins, and certain dreams,
None so shining as my bride.
I watch her nimble, darting thimble-thrust,
Her inward smile,
Her easy breast;
I read of heroes and am not oppressed.
Her belly's gradual, presaging swell
Eclipses Everest.

Night-Watch

The slaked man lies across me.
   Him and his snoring
I carry up and down, among my breathing.
   The bed has stopped, and doesn't toss me.

The clock, with shocked tick-ticking,
   Makes for the morning
To kettle, tea and trousers;
   But I am learning
Awake, adark, over his heedless breathing,
   This name of mother.

The Guests

(A woman speaks on two occasions of her life -
pregnancy and on learning of a malignant growth)

Guest of my body,
Silent sir,
Fruitful deformity
And interloper
Between my love and me,
I wait for your
Quirk and acknowledging,
The revolution that unseats you is
My crowning.

Guest of my body,
Silent fire
Deforming and devouring,
You, usurper
And knife-outwitter,
Tissue-blossom,
You are the truer
Comrade, son and brother,
Darkly embracing,
Always companioning
Without rebellion
My flesh to its dissolving.

Aubade In Winter

The icicles above our window-sill
Are sharp and hard as any woman's will,
Lie close, my love, lie close, and thaw me still.

Stroking the dark, and curling with the blood,
Lovers by touch, in stillness understood,
A silent wife, the proverb says, is good.

The cock that splits the curtain of the night
Reports the first reconnaissance of light.
Take cover, love. The day is dynamite.

Utter no mutter, reach for no alarm.
Roll over, O my love, and drown the dawn
In one warm, calm, wet, world-engulfing yawn.

Knitting

A pullover, please, for winter.

Take the single strand and roll it into a ball.
Slowly unroll,
Twine round fingers,
Pinion onto probing needles.

Knit one, purl one, knit one, purl one, till
The edge is steady and the waist is grasped,
Then
One row plain and one row purl, until
We begin to shape the arm-holes,
Shape
The single strand to a pair of purposeful
Responsible arms and shoulders.

Decrease, knit two together. Carefully, carefully;
Best to write down where you are on a piece of paper.

Now for the neck, where the collar holds the voice,
Where the head emerges, blazing,
Where the individual, sharp and sole for himself,
Thrusts himself into my standard, concocted pattern.

However quick, however deft the fingers,
However
Snug the cosy woollen prison,
He will distort it with his frenzied living,
His slump of sleeping and his stains of being.

The pattern stands only a moment perfect.
Next winter, socks.

Couples

1

Their every movement turns to honey,
Their lips pour wine.
This is once, once only.

2

To every act its consequence.
A lather of children,
Talking, laughing, jumping, sucking toffee—
And the progenitors, carrying all the bundles.

3

Everything he touches turns to money.
His wife weeps, under the sheet
Her golden breasts are cold.

4

No flies on her.
He, on the contrary, collects
Beetles and moths, whatever creeps or crawls,
Extinguishable creatures.

Hanging Out The Wash

Our garments, air-inflated, big with wind,
Dance their caricatures on the flogging line.

The teeth of wooden and plastic pegs hold down
Our woollies to be raped by a screaming north-easter.

The sun assaults their colouring: a shirt
Is crucified in ice: knickers distended, pregnant.

Strung
Between house and garden,
Tied
To a sagging, flapping line

They are caricatures—oh, surely!

Look, it's beginning to rain, I must bring them in
Till, warm and dry and tame, they fit us again.

Assassin

The year went past, in crimson: one lone gold
Tree, bored and enrobed, still held on—
Rearguard security for the royal party.

I raised my rifle: and lowered it again
Unused, quietly. Nobody was noticing,
Everyone else was attending to the procession.

The position was perfect: the aim, accurate;
Arrest certain, execution probable.
I could have released the irreversible blood

From a small hole in the centre of the forehead.
I triggered certainty with shaking fingers
And hesitated: and routine took over.

Everything is reprieved till the following spring.
Hiding my rifle under the autumn leaves,
I go back to work, with the other failed assassins.

Winter In Lodgings

Mr. Pritchard was the first to pass away.
Out late, wet, and got the pneumonia
On the top of his bronchitis,
In all that cold he reached a high temperature
And was cremated, last January.
They put the remains in a very nice little jar
But nobody quite seems to know just whereabouts it is.
They say he was just a wee bit too fond of the bottle,
Poor soul, in a jar, pickled at last.

Mrs. Ledbury, she was more romantic,
She had everything fixed up,
She was laid to rest in peace in her native village,
She lies in the Midland clay beside the by-pass
Motionless, without her knitting-needles.
Strangers can now go past her unidentified,
The telly has lost the spice of her disapproval,
We no longer know what she thinks about simply everything.

Miss Kelly is one of a number in North London.
We mean to go up and find her and take some flowers
On a fine Sunday in summer,
For she was nice, Miss Kelly, and fond of flowers
And babies and kittens and calendars. We hope Heaven
Will be just what she fancied. Killed by a motor-bike.
Not a very nice death for a ladylike person.

With Mr. Wilson, it was Anno Domini,
And took much longer.
Doing his crossword puzzles up to the last
He began to find the clues a little beyond him,

Never mind, he said, we'll get the solution tomorrow,
Which he finally did.
                    Yes, it's been quite a winter,
To think about, over the evening cocoa,
With a kind of satisfaction.

In Retirement

Widowed of my own image
That shone from fellow faces
I watch from envious window
The men whose energies at morning
Are sucked towards the safe corporeal city.

Young men who run on rails, bereft
Of personal intention, don't condemn
The older one immobile in a chair!
You are the playthings: I the pioneer
Of white Antarctica, bloodless and bare.

Song Before Sunrise

She knocked like a woman at the door of my age.
I shouted out "Come in". In came hot milk,
Comforting to a stomach, good to sleep with
For an old man, failing, in a wide bed.

The moon confronts me like an empty plate.
I get the girl to set the curtains right.
It's larger in the dark. Nothing is shrunk.
I melt the clock and pour the minutes out.

The sky gets up at four, puts on its white,
Solidifies. The busy birds begin
To chip away my eighty years of sleep.
I buried the sun so often. Now she comes

Whom I refused, the once, the only sun.
Crippled with sleep or raging in my work
I had no time for sunrise. Time has come.

Unpractised in the opening of the eyes
And blind and clumsy in the waking sun
I go a virgin to the bed of light.

Late Fall

About the height of noon
The manless creatures come to take the sun
This one we call a butterfly
Has landed on my hand, I don't know why.

Some warmth or texture or suspected sap
Inveigled it into this possible trap.

Top-heavy: ticklish; nourished on a weed,
Dotted and dashed with signals I can't read,

It comes in black, white, orange, blue and brown,
Topples a moment and settles blandly down.

Calm in the sun that made today its day.

Be off, you.
Do whatever it is you have to do,

I do not kill, nor spare, nor pardon.
There is no god walking in this garden.

Death Of A Gardener

An old man, taking the last turning
Towards home, collapsed like a marriage;
The ambulance came along, clanging,
The hospital was white, unhopeful,

And the flowers came in all round him, sweet-smelling,
All his life he was a breeder of flowers.

Now they huddle to watch his dragging of breathing.
He knows what yellow clay attends the roots of flowers,
What humus, what passage of worms, what frosty crumblings,
What sun's trumpeting calls up their transience,

And how, when they come to decay, no-one is watching or grieving
As the cold falls
And colour drains away and form stiffens.

Cut back, cut back now, bonfire and tidy,
Dig in the riches of decomposition,
Ash, bone, husk, droppings, leavings,

The lights coming on indoors, the books open,
The seed catalogue spread for another summer.

A Very Cold Winter

                   So cold, the wool
Cannot keep the sheep.
              Trees, in their tinkling skins,
Are leafless and complete.
                 The songbirds' beaks
Are sealed; so cold, their feet
Freeze to the twig, their lyric inches topple
Hard over fast
            to the softly burying snow.
Feathers to ice: and weeping turns
                    to ice.
Icicles bar the windows, pointing fingers
Longward and downward,
            where the feeding green
Skulks underground,
          where only the mice make merry
In their runagate caves.
             Life-size men in bed,
In the cold's embrace, between their shuddering sheets,
Cannot beget their hot impulsive kind.

Now there will never again be midges: now
The bound god rigid on the mountain hangs.

The puddle split to stars, where feet were put,
And the feet are few, now.
              The night knocks,

The night creaks and settles, huge with stars,
The burning points of cold.
             Our glistening shroud
Stiffens around us: we rehearse the stars'
Inanimate calm. We join the dead bright shiners.

We find no reason for any other hope,
Coldly reasoning here, in the last of the heat,
Between this heart-beat and that, hesitant, heart-beat.

If the starched land capitulates to thaw
Tomorrow,
Waking to drip and drizzle, shall I be glad
Of the brown trickle, the gurgling, giggling mud,
The breeding squalor, dull, tepid and good?

The Last Of The Rain

The rain has almost stopped; and still the drops
Ping and smack from the edge of the soused thatch,
Water dawdles and maunders in the channels
Of the wrinkling road, and all the unsettled hill
Strains at ditches, fuddles in gutters, erupts
In sudden springs, and sticks in the straight throat
Of grating and drain, a tumid humus of weed,
Leavings of green; slime; and kneeling straws
Sucked from the stubble; somersaulted twigs,
Bark, husk, rubble and dust now water-winged,
Voluble, sociable now in the fluent flood.

Wellington and galosh, tyre-splash and hoof
Pock and print the various mobile mud,
But the sliding wile of silt
Drips back into its rut, and there sinks;
Detritus droops; sand settles; the murky clears;
And all the turbid rush
Takes on tranquillity, and holds the sky
Shining, in water colour,
Calmly reflects the jewelled intangible air
On an undercoat of mud, as the earth must,
Stretched as it is on the determining rocks
From face of clay to queer unvisited core;
Whatever opaque impasto swirls above
—Alive in stench and daub, slither and crunch,
Worm, bacteria, weed-seed, harvest-seed—
The centre's drab and hard.

The superficial rain dances and sings,
Sobers and steadies, seeps and carries on down

To manufacture coal-and-diamond stuff
Or sharpen rot, where only darkness is
And carcases, and promises
That make men mine the pit, and die of the dead weight
Of earth and water mixed.
Rivers run underground, as waters can,
Where wits trip and the will chills and the mere throat
Falters and chokes; the centre has no voice.

The superficial rain dances and sings
And so do I, do I, do I. Do I?
The centre has no voice.

The cows come close to the house
Heavy with milk and rain,
Breathing out moist reproaches, shuffling muck,
On the wrong cold side of the wall where warm and dry
I
Sit at a desk and write the praise of wet
In the blood's decline, while the running of the rain
Stops, perhaps permanently. Anyhow, stops.

Song Of The Late Afternoon

To be where the white horse rouses
   Up from the den beneath,
To live in their wild houses,
   To feel their fiery teeth
Snap on the flying word . . .

How far has the sun-dial crept?
   What news of the bee?
(Roots moved: I slept)
   Has the thistle unpowdered now?
I cannot see . . .

To be where droop rides heavy
   And creak is king,
To dread the draughts of the black door
   Closing, opening,
To live safe and steady,

To flinch and finger-spy
   When the white hooves go by
Gallop, gallop who may,
   Ears must have a stop,
A shade for the eye,
   Thwarted anatomy
Sober and slump must lie
   Still . . .

Still
When the white hooves go by
   They shake the clay
And the hairs of the neck stand up
   (Still)
At the flight of the word.

On Coming To The Woods

These will be my last words,
No need for words in the woods
In the midst of width. The lift
And strike of bud from twig,
Sprung without urge of words,

Hurries the summer to glut,
Flourishes foliage, lets
Crisply in winter slip
Leaves that sag to a wet

Wading of colour plucked
From the rubbed and fretted woods,
Worked by a wind in stress,
Scorched by the first of frost.

I walk, in the wind's wake,
Kept by a coat from the cold,
By a beat of heart from the earth,
Blurring my feet with leaves,
Shuffling metre and stress,
Hearing the seasons breathe.

Having known the oak when old
Toppled into the mud
And the air bare where it stood,
I have taken my leave of words
That wither in wilderness
And come to no humble good
Feeding another's roots
Warming another's hearth.

I have come to the end of words
And live on the verge of the woods.

Turning Out The Mattresses

When we were turning out the mattresses,
Fooling and laughing and heaving and calling across,
I suddenly remembered: you aren't here.
And stood, shaken to pieces by the loss;
As we were turning out the mattresses,
I had to go on. Irreparable distresses,
Eloquent elegies, the waste of tears
Aren't for women with supper to get and all.
It was only a year ago, the funeral
To the time of turning out the mattresses.

This bit of paper's your memorial.

Harry Chambers / Peterloo Poets

'Harry Chambers's *Peterloo Poets* series, an offshoot of his editing of *Phoenix*, shows the same persistence and flair that marks the magazine.' **The Times Literary Supplement**

'A series which looks set to rival the almost-legendary *Fantasy* and *Marvell Press* imprints.' **The Use Of English**

'There is a consistency about this series, edited by Harry Chambers, which is admirable.' **British Book News**

'A tribute to small-press pertinacity.' *Alan Brownjohn,* **The New Statesman**

'A remarkable venture.' **Tribune**

'For quite a few years Harry Chambers has been working in the north west of England, without unnecessary fuss and with commendable energy, taste and enthusiasm, to bring the work of unfashionable, neglected or undervalued poets before a larger reading public.' *Vernon Scannell,* **Ambit**

Free catalogue available.

8 CAVENDISH ROAD, HEATON MERSEY, STOCKPORT, CHESHIRE SK4 3DN

NEW ADDRESS

HARRY CHAMBERS/PETERLOO POETS
Treovis Farm Cottage, Upton Cross, Liskeard, Cornwall PL14 5BQ

Elma Mitchell. Born 1919 at Airdrie in Scotland. A professional librarian, she was educated at Prior's Field School and Somerville College, Oxford, where she read English. She has also worked in broadcasting, publishing, journalism etc., in London, but now lives in Somerset and works as a freelance writer and translator. Her first serious poem was published in *P.E.N. New Poems, 1967*, edited by Harold Pinter, John Fuller and Peter Redgrove. *The Times Literary Supplement*, reviewing this anthology, wrote: "the most enjoyable and immediately striking poem is by an entirely unknown contributor, Elma Mitchell. Her 'Thoughts After Ruskin' deserves wide notice". In 1969 Elma Mitchell was the winner of the £100 Camden Festival Poetry Book Prize with a group of poems, *Seasons And Enquiries*, chosen from anonymous submission by judges C. Day Lewis, Anthony Thwaite and Edward Lucie-Smith. The following year she was runner-up with another group of unpublished poems, *18 Ways Of Being A Woman*. Poems from both these groups plus more recent poems are included in the present volume. *The Poor Man in The Flesh* is a belated first full collection.